EXPLORE *and* DISCOVER *your* PURPOSE

EXPLORE *and*
DISCOVER
your PURPOSE

6 Steps to Uncover
YOUR *Dream Career*

MARLO ANDERSEN

NEW YORK

LONDON • NASHVILLE • MELBOURNE • VANCOUVER

EXPLORE *and* DISCOVER *your* PURPOSE
6 Steps to Uncover YOUR *Dream Career*

© 2020 **MARLO ANDERSEN**

Published in New York, New York, by Morgan James Publishing in partnership with Difference Press. Morgan James is a trademark of Morgan James, LLC. www.MorganJamesPublishing.com

ISBN 978-1-64279-446-5 paperback
ISBN 978-1-64279-447-2 eBook
Library of Congress Control Number: 2019931152

Cover Design by:
Rachel Lopez
www.r2cdesign.com

Interior Design by:
Bonnie Bushman
The Whole Caboodle Graphic Design

In an effort to support local communities, raise awareness and funds, Morgan James Publishing donates a percentage of all book sales for the life of each book to Habitat for Humanity Peninsula and Greater Williamsburg.

Get involved today! Visit
www.MorganJamesBuilds.com

For Rhett and our children.

TABLE OF CONTENTS

INTRODUCTION

*"It's the possibility of having a dream
come true that makes life interesting."*
—Paulo Coelho

This book is about more than finding a career that earns a great income and works with your schedule. It is about the adventure of carving out your own life the way you imagine it. It is about uncovering a passion that has deeper meaning to you and supports your values in life. We are talking about possessing the foresight to explore and discover your purpose and then manifesting that into your dream career. There is nothing more beautiful, liberating, and powerful than a person who is honest in asking this of themselves and who is true in following their heart and putting up the binoculars to find the right help to get them where they want to go.

Just imagine. You are living the life of your dreams because you got an inspiration and followed it. You trusted yourself. Each day has led to this season in your life. Motherhood has been your first work. Now there is a stirring in your heart to pursue your second work and find a passion you can call your own. You know there is something more, and like the woman on the cover of this book, you can see what calls you with greater clarity.

Motherhood is a big sacrifice that pays over and over in the years to come. Women are so powerful. We hold the love of the world in our hands and in our hearts, shaping the future generations. We have the right to find what we are capable of and to expand ourselves. We have the right to explore all the corners of our inner world, have fun in the process, and discover our truest selves. We have the right to feel that we have continually more to offer. We are mothers. We are priceless. We are much, much more.

Choose Yourself

It is true that you can become whatever it is you desire. The reverse is also true. We can be stuck when doubt, anxiety, and fear overtake us. However, the proof that you are made to do something amazing is found in the desire itself.

After desire, we work on belief. We could ask someone else what it is they believe we ought to be. However, I have never seen that work. The complete story of you is only found when you do the personal work to uncover it. The more intentional and mindful your approach to your personal work, the greater and deeper the results. These personal transformative results translate into the career you are looking for.

Terry Orlick, world-renowned Olympic high-performance coach, once said, "The heart of human excellence often begins to beat when you discover a pursuit that absorbs you, frees you, challenges you, or gives you a sense of meaning, joy, or passion." That beat of the heart is found in the genuine pursuit of uncovering your true identity and your true self. There is no substitute to diving deep into your inner world in order to expand your dreams into further and unseen places. You hold the keys to your life.

I am excited you are here. Welcome!

Chapter 1

TRUST YOUR
HEART'S DESIRE

*"Once you believe in yourself
and see your soul as divine and precious,
you'll automatically be converted
to a being who can create miracles."*
—Wayne W. Dyer

As a work of art in motion, you are constantly evolving and shaping. Take a moment and listen to your own story. What does it sound like in your own ears? What would you tell yourself about how you are feeling today? Write that down where you can come back to it.

Trust and listen to yourself. Trusting in one's own self is a remarkable ability. It is when you feel that gut knowing or that warmth in your heart. It is an internal recognition of your truth. All that you need is inside you; however, the not-so-easy trick is knowing how to uncover it. While the details of the journey may look different for some of us, the principles of how to get there are universal.

Having a Servant's Heart

There is nothing selfish about wanting to find your gifts so you can grow and give more to others. The choice in your life to bear or adopt and raise children was not easy. Patience and putting yourself aside is the order of the day in the life of a mother. Taking a shower was a treat, and being alone to go to the bathroom was rare. Anyone have a baby or toddler on their lap while on the toilet? You are the one making sure the house is in running order, the kids get to their lessons on time, homework is done, and instruments are practiced. It is a common story in the life of a stay-at-home mom.

Think of all the tears you have lovingly wiped away, all the life lessons you have taught when friend problems would arise, and all the times you were the self-esteem cheerleader when tryouts or a test didn't go well. And if we had a dollar for each diaper we have changed, we could buy our own small island.

Like you, I would not change the opportunity to raise my kids. Raising my five kids has been the most fulfilling experience of my life, one that's available for only a short time. What a great life experience it is to be a mom. Each day brings its own challenges and its own rewards. If you are reading this, my bet is you have a servant's heart. You gave your all to your children and now you want to expand your reach. Now, you feel something calling you. My guess is that you feel like it is coming soon.

In my experience as a transformation coach and healer, I see every day the fact that most people do not know how powerful they truly are. Your innate capacity to make a difference in the world is an eternal truth. With honesty, curiosity, and perseverance, you can find exactly what you are seeking, and much more that you did not know was available to you, if you are open to finding it.

Celebrate this warrior inside who wants to know what she is made of. There are many of us who share this same story. Have you ever been called a firecracker or stubborn, strong-willed, or anything similar? Believe me, it's a compliment!

You Are Not Alone

You are never alone. There are many other kindred spirit stay-at-home moms with a life continuation plan, as well as many who share your questions and concerns:

"I have been out of the workforce for so long; what do I have to offer?"

"I don't want to just go back to the old thing I did, but I would have no idea what the next thing could be."

"I'm terrified and feel like I have no place to start."

"I'm a little embarrassed to tell many people of my desire for a career. What if they doubt me? Even worse, what if I try and fail?"

"What if I end up regretting my job choice and get stuck in something I don't enjoy?"

"I don't want to be stuck in a schedule with a traditional job, but creating my own business sounds overwhelming."

"I don't want to just be doing busy work. I want this thing to really count in my life."

What kind of evidence do you have to support these problems and fears? Let's reverse these statements and evaluate the opposite scenario.

"My fresh perspective and energy in the workforce will offer much to the world."

"Because I have changed so much in the last several years, I am proactive in discovering my talents and have a new, clear direction."

"I'm excited about this new phase in life and consider it an adventure."

"I confidently share my heart's desire with those who love me. I have confidence in myself and know that there is no way to fail; there is only learning and succeeding.

"Because I did my due diligence of discovering my deepest self, I can trust I am on the right path."

"With my newfound purpose in life, I am finding all the support I need to create my dream career that is flexible and actually gives me more energy than I have ever had."

"Each day has meaning and joy, because I am living my unique purpose. I have a deep internal motivation to build my business because I am in charge and am the creator. "

Just as you could find evidence for the truth of your biggest fears, what is the evidence that the positive is true? Yes, you can find valid and convincing reason for the positive.

What if I told you that there is no such thing as an absolute truth about any of these statements? Your life results will follow what you invest in it and only the direction you give it.

Or don't give it.

Have a Burning Desire

Think of the first time you remember wanting something, I mean really wanted something. Maybe it was to buy a certain item. Your parents may have told you to pay for it yourself. So you started saving up all your baby sitting and birthday money. The day came when you could buy it. It meant so much more than if someone had handed it to you. But you earned it. You created your own dream come true.

Now what if that thing were an expanded talent. You wanted to make the dance team, the soccer team, or the debate team, or you wanted to get an A in the toughest class in school. That sort of want is what puts you out there. It puts you on the front line. You found the place in yourself to go out and try. Trying, making the effort, and doing our best is enough.

The point is not whether you made this happen. Maybe it took another round or two; maybe it never worked. That is OK. The important part is the honest effort of a heart on fire. Strength is gained. Character is developed. Determination is practiced. These are what we gain. This is what we take with us and no one can do that for us or take it away. Think. What did you gain? What was the reward? I bet that no matter the result, you would never trade the experience. All of these things have made you who you are today, and no one can take that away from you. In my experience with people and as a coach, it is the souls with the most determination to persevere who gain all that they are looking for. And in every single case, these focused individuals find much, much more than they thought they were setting out to find.

Chapter 2
THERE IS SOMETHING MORE

*"Each person has the divine right
to see themselves as God sees them."*
—Marlo Andersen

Opportunity is all we have. Each person has the opportunity to learn from all things. It is a way of life to choose to learn and grow from all things wonderful, difficult, and in between. We are all standing where we are today because of the choices we made to learn.

As young girl–chapter 1, version 1 of myself–I envisioned both having a family and expanding myself further into having something to do for work. That idea never left me. It was like I had a double vision of my life: to have a lot of kids and to later have a career. I loved it. It was a dream I kept alive. At the time, it didn't matter what that career was. I just wanted to do something that was mine. I wanted to have that feeling of independence and moving forward. I wanted to make my own money. I wanted to know that no matter what happened in life, I would have my thing.

Coming Clean About My Toilet Obsession

As a mom I'm sure you have cleaned a lot of toilets. I had many years of clean toilet obsession. My friends knew about it, and they had a lot of fun with it as word got around. Sounds funny, right? But it was true. I cleaned all toilets in my house each day and some more than once. I cleaned my entire bathroom each night before bed. I got really, really fast at it. One time my friend was sick, so I cleaned for her one day. Her eyes popped open at how sparkling everything was and in such a short period of time. She mentions it still, and it has been over twenty years ago.

My cleaning extended to baseboards, walls, and cabinet fronts in some way daily. It took minutes, and it was very satisfying. I did not know this at the time, but at one point, I realized that there were two reasons why I did this. One, I could do it better and faster each time. This made me feel like

I was getting in something that could otherwise be ignored, but in under five minutes, I had it done. I was the master. It was like always having the extras done that makes you feel like you are ahead.

The second one was that while I was cleaning, I had a moment of brain wave change, or something like that, and I could tap into some sort of inspiration. I felt it most while cleaning a toilet. It was just me, in this tiny room with this toilet, and there is nothing else going on. I can remember several toilet inspirations (crazy, right?) that got me through questions I had or gave me a direction. Interestingly enough, these little sparks of genius were only about me and my personal journey. It was like God was showing me that I was still recognized as a separate person outside of my responsibility as a mother. I felt remembered.

These reminders of my unique identity took me to so many places that I could not have gone if I were not on a menial task like cleaning toilets. There's something to having your head under a toilet bowl that make things real. I think it is in the humility of it all. If I were being toted around on a golden pillow like the Queen of Sheba, I would have too many distractions. But being on your hands and knees cleaning something that no one aspires to do grounds you in a way. It's like I am just me. I am a person who has things to do. I am not self-important. I am not haughty. I am down-to-earth. I am willing to be of service in a simple way. I will clean this toilet and do it well.

Those moments of humility that allow for personal awareness create a channel for God to have a few moments with you. You are in a place to receive. You are willing to listen. You don't put yourself above others. That is when the opportunity comes to hear your inner voice and what God has to say.

I still clean my own toilets. Sometimes a housekeeper helps here and there, on and off, but much of the job is still mine. I have my kids clean their own bathrooms. It teaches them the same lesson. Once anyone thinks they are above something, selfishness appears and light disappears. I have even found cleaning supplies in gas station restrooms and in public buildings and cleaned them.

I also find my inner voice while walking, falling asleep, doing dishes, formally praying, meditating, talking with someone in an honest way, reading—the list goes on and on. The more you practice being open as a way of life, the more God can help you. However, I never find it while in resistance, in fear, in frustration, or in arrogance. That is a closed door to moving ahead in life.

• • • • •

Ballet was my passion (OK, my obsession) growing up, and I pursued contemporary dance as my degree at university. While I was passionate about dance, I chose to not dance professionally but to have a baby. My heart was called to start my family. Still, instead of performing professionally for a living, I raised children and taught dance from my years in college and continued teaching for twenty-three years. I taught ballet, contemporary choreography and composition, creative dance, jazz, and other styles to people of all ages, starting with children of eighteen months to adults of fifty years. I was at home in my heart in the dance studio. It was my place. I connected to my students of all ages and levels. They were in my heart. I rejoiced exceedingly as each would improve and discover themselves in and through dance. It was a real triumph.

At one point, I opened my own studio which I branded, marketed (this could be a whole book unto itself). I wrote curriculum there and hired the best teachers, as well as choreographed, directed, and wrote trophy-winning performances. And it was a lot of work. My family and the people who knew me well saw me collapsing. But I was determined. Soon enough I had my studio running and humming like a well-oiled machine. Then once I got it to that place, a whisper in my head said, "The dance studio is not it." You have got to be kidding me!

I was confused. I always want to work with God's direction, but this did not seem fair! And what else was I supposed to do? Could I be as good at anything else? What if this is a big mistake. In all humility, I admit I was resistant. It made no sense. I tried to figure it out. Each time I thought of selling it, I got nauseous and dizzy and would have to sit down. I had put blood, sweat, and tears (all literal) into making this grow. My ambition was to expand and have more than one location. I saw myself as Miss Marlo teaching at age eighty-eight.

My entire wish was for children, and adults, to learn to know who they are and to be able to be free thinkers so they can make their mark and live to their fullest potential. My heart would burst as I saw this happening in class and on the stage. I saw great transformation in my students. And I put my heart into providing it for them.

However, if I was going to have the wisdom to be on a path of true purpose in life, I had to listen to what the universe was telling me. I sold my studio and got help to uncover where I was supposed to go next. Through a course of transformation work, I discovered miracles inside me I never knew existed. My purpose, in simple terms, is why I write this book.

It is my hope that each person releases limitations and uncovers the truth of their power and potential. Each human has the right to the opportunity to find a deepened purpose in life in a personally supportive and worthwhile career or ambition, one that you love and call your own. It's true freedom and it is a journey that is worth the trip. Each day I wake up and say, "God, please put me to use. What is it that I can do today?"

Oftentimes, well, all the time, a new adventure is a little intimidating. Blocks come forward, and I eliminate them. That is when I clean a toilet (just kidding).

We all have blocks. It is inevitable to run into them. If there were no blocks, we would all have all we could ever dream of on a continual basis and not be searching for more. Most of these internal barriers are extremely stubborn, complex, and interwoven with other barriers and cannot be willed away by the mind.

· · · · ·

When I first was married at age twenty-two, my husband and I were both still in school. My husband had a summer job on a drilling rig. It was hard work, but it paid well. As newlyweds, I followed him to Elko, Nevada, for three weeks. We were in a motel room with no kitchen. I was alone all day while he worked. I craved finding something I could do to make any sort of money. I asked the hotel if they would hire me to make beds or something while I stayed there. Three weeks is no time to find any sort of employment. I put my head to work and racked my brain on what I could do. I got the idea to walk to all the casinos in the area. They give out free orange juice (I skipped the vodka) and a free token to everyone each day.

I collected one dollar from each casino. It took me most of the day to make the trips to all the casinos. I then would walk to the grocery store and use my income to buy dinner ingredients. I then walked back to the hotel and cooked on a hotplate on the floor. I did this for the three weeks we were there. This is not to demonstrate how to make eight dollars a day; my hopes for you are much larger than that. It is to show that in any circumstance, no matter how bleak or limiting, if one has the will to make a difference in a situation, the answer will appear. And when one is willing to do the harder things, it will be made easier. Greater ways will be shown because of willingness to work. Out of willingness to be of service, a way will be shown 100 percent of the time.

· · · · ·

If you are feeling in your heart that there is something more for you, believe it. There is. It is waiting for you. It wants you to find it. It is your future self calling to you in the now.

This is where 100 percent pure honesty comes in. Do I want to take this step in my life or do I not? Only you can make that judgment for your life. It's not the life of anyone else but yours. Life will always keep going. Each year will come to the next. In twenty years, who is the person you want to be? How do you want to be giving of yourself?

I promise you, when you are living in your true purpose and living to serve with your highest gifts and talents, that is when you are in the place to give the best of yourself. Nothing else can match that.

Life will energize you to a level that only those who are in that place can experience. Health and well-being improves, you look younger, you wake up with energy, you sleep better. Other people notice when someone is in their power. It is very attractive. It is enlightening and encouraging to see someone shine from inside when they are enjoying how they are spending their day and their life. You have limitless amount of love and energy to give. Life has great meaning. It feels amazing to exist in your body.

If you could see your power and your ability to influence the world for good, you would not believe what you are seeing. So few ever learn who they really are and what is available to them. Those who are willing to invest in themselves to explore and discover their purpose are the leaders and lifeblood of humanity.

Chapter 3

IT'S ALWAYS WORTH THE JOURNEY

"It doesn't interest me what you do for a living.
I want to know what you ache for and if you
dare to dream of meeting your heart's longing."
—Oriah Mountain Dreamer

The mark of a career that resonates with you is one that gives you undeniable clarity, joy, and a sense of purpose. It works with your energy. You wake up excited. You don't mind a little inconvenience from time to time because you have the bigger vision that this is something you are doing out of choice and out of love for yourself and for others. Let there not be any discouragement, regret, or resentment. Let there only be gratitude that you are serving in your new career with meaning and passion.

Passion is required. Without passion, you are just filling time. It is going through the motions and waiting for the clock to signal you are done. Looking forward to Friday is great and natural. It means you have a fun life. But looking forward to Friday to have relief from work is a bad sign. And Sunday evening depression is even worse. Vow to yourself that you will do better than setting yourself up for that. Don't give in to convenience. If it is necessary to get a job and you have an opportunity, by all means take it, do your best at it, and be grateful. It will be rewarding to know you are giving all of yourself to something that is necessary for you for the time being.

However, don't stop dreaming. Don't stop looking if that job is not the dream destination. As you work at home or at a bridge job, keep your mind alive. Be motivated to give, love, and put your best into something. Have a real reason for working and searching. Be open to what is speaking to you.

I love writing creative stories with a spiritual meaning. It gives me joy. In this book, all the stories I have written have fictional characters. I will share a few with you to make this time we have together more meaningful and insightful–and a little more fun! I want to share with you the possibilities of how this journey of exploring and discovering your new career can look for you. The first story, "Worth the Journey," came to me a few years ago while in a quiet moment of meditation and contemplation on personal growth.

In "Worth the Journey," you will see the woman moving along observing houses. Each house represents how we can choose to live our lives. Notice the last house had a humble exterior, but the simplicity is deceiving. Inside there is a spiritual journey that is available to all but only found by those who are willing to keep going. It is all too easy to stop and feel as if you are done here. It is the reward of those who have an instinct and desire to continue on their spiritual journey that find what others could only think was impossible. For the two other women, this level of depth was completely invisible. Take time to internalize and absorb this as you read it. Where do you see yourself in the process and where would you like to go?

Below is a story I wrote that explores this very question.

Worth the Journey

A woman walked by a house. It was pleasant and comfortable. She walked in and saw a cozy room with a fire. The view was limited and the yard was tight, but it was convenient. "This will do." She smiled. So, she stayed and stopped her journey.

A second woman strode by. She saw the first house—agreeable and cute, but she continued on to the next one. It was grander than the first from the outside. And the inside bore its proof.

It had a large foyer, a grand piano, and a winding stair case. The view was improved from the first house, and the yard was large. She felt a little smarter than the other woman having chosen this more spacious house. So, she stayed and stopped her journey there.

A third woman passed by. She saw the first house with its pretty shutters and small view. The first woman invited her in, but more curious than comfortable, she continued on.

Next, she saw the large house with its fancy porches and higher view. The second woman encouraged her to join her. The rooms of this house promised luxury and benefits.

More curious than satisfied, the third woman was drawn to a third house at the end of the street.

It was sturdy, fresh, and clean. From the front, it looked plain and humble. However, a sign hung that read, "Home Sweet Home." Intrigued, the third woman began toward this house.

Both the first and the second woman were concerned as she moved toward the third house. "Do not go there! Look at it. It is far too simple. There are no shutters or beautiful porch. The inside will be just as plain. You will regret it. You will see."

However, the third woman—more courageous than fearful—approached the third house. The first two women laughed and went into their houses to go about their business.

She cracked open the door. It opened to a long hall that continued back for over 150 feet. It appeared simple. A few others had been curious like her and opened the front door, but they saw little and turned away.

More hopeful than she was discouraged, she continued through the long hall. At the back there was another door. She opened it. In there was a massive library—books on every subject possible. "Stay here," she thought, "and I can learn everything there is to know about the world. I will be educated and independent."

But more honest of heart than she was convinced, she continued through the library.

At the end of the library, she found another door. Behind this door was a vast and spacious marbled area. Many great philosophers roamed the area.

"Stay here," she thought, "and I will know the secrets of the universe."

But more humble than she was important, she continued through the colossal and tremendous marbled room.

After traveling for what seemed a full day, she got to the end of the white, marbled expanse. No door this time—it just dropped off.

She hung her toes off the ledge. Before her was just space. There were no floor, no ceiling, no walls.

A man was floating in the space, he invited her to step out into his waiting hand.

More trusting than she was frightened, she placed her foot onto the man's outreached palm.

No longer did she think of the houses, or the library or the marble room.

There was only her.

She was aware of only herself—Her True Self.

The soul that is unique—Her Soul.

The soul that was created with a grand purpose behind it. The purpose that is uniquely hers alone.

Bathing her cells in the memory of her true identity. She was finally home.

This was worth the journey.

The end.

It is each person's divine right to choose how they want to live, as long as one does not intentionally seek to do harm to the development of another. So, with that gift, let's take a minute and see what each choice may look like in the real world. Here, I ask you to begin making a decision about which "house" speaks to you. With no decision or vision, we always default to the path of least resistance and live life by circumstance. By the end of the book, we will come back to this place, and you will have the opportunity to have a clarity on which metaphorical, spiritual "house" you choose to live in.

The first stop the woman makes on her journey is represented as a small cottage. By the way, I have a little fetish with cozy spaces and would love to vacation in a little hobbit house. (A quirky dream of mine.) There is little to no risk in acquiring this small cottage and not much had to be done in preparation. There is little to no view of the landscape or surroundings. It bears little upkeep. How do you think this translates to life path?

Although this is nothing against lovely, homey cottages, it is a metaphor for taking the path of least resistance. Little stretching is needed. The lack of view is symbolic of not seeing far in terms of spiritual eyes and personal insights. Notice how she stopped at the first house she saw and had no desire to see what else could be available to her.

Seeing what else is available comes first just by having the desire and intention to ask—asking yourself, asking God, asking the universe what other options there for you are and what you will need to do to be ready to recognize and utilize them when they show up. It can just start with a desire to learn more.

The second house was enjoyed by the next woman. She was willing to take a longer stride, and once she saw the two-story house, she was satisfied. It had a much larger and expansive interior, nicer furnishings and had a farther-reaching view. More work was required, and she was happy to do it. She enjoyed the amenities, and all the different rooms offered something else for her in her life, giving her the variety and depth she wanted. Plus, the view offered a little insight here and there. How do you see this as a metaphor for finding a dream career?

The point to be made here is that she stopped thinking that all that could be available to her was here. What else could she want for? This two-story house is pretty darn comfortable. And here is the deception: if something is painted as more wonderful than you currently have, and you stop there by assumption, you will always be under your full potential. The two-story house doesn't work for a dreamer. It becomes uncomfortable one day.

Next, we have the small, unassuming house at the end with the sign that read, "Home Sweet Home." First, I want to address why I made it such a simple structure, even less cute and appealing than the cottage at the front of the road. You see, doing our deeper work to find the richest piece of life is not often the glamorous or obvious. It is quiet, internal, and only shared and understood by those who have the desire to uncover what lies beneath the surface. Notice the two neighboring women misunderstanding, discouraging, and even mocking her. Have you ever felt that come up in your life when you have shared your desire to grow further? (I have.)

The rooms and expanses in the third house at the end of the road represent our journey to keep going. As we come to a new room of personal understanding, there is another room with deeper understanding and growth behind it waiting for you to enter. This is the journey to ourselves.

The sign on the third house reads, "Home Sweet Home." This symbolizes the feeling you get when you decide to discover your true self. It feels like you are finally coming home.

The six steps in this book prepare you to go the depth of the back of the house. Like the simplicity of the exterior of the third house, the concepts are simple. It is the execution and progression in it that is the work. It is also the grand reward that pays infinitely in return.

Reaching High

It is fairly easy to find a job, if you are not too picky. And if you only wanted a job, you would already have one and not be reading this book. If I am right, the thought of taking the least common denominator option is not your idea of a thrilling life. Living a life by precedence, or by what just happens easily around you, is not that exciting. Instead, it's a little depressing.

The six steps I lay out in this book are the foundational stepping-stones to uncover and peel away the illusions to reveal the true self and your new dream career.

6 Steps to Uncover Your Dream Career

In this book, you will learn that there are six foundational steps to attaining this level of fulfillment and purpose in life. Each chapter will outline, discuss, and inspire hungry people in search of their true gifts and purpose in life. These steps are not about simply choosing something and then plug and play. This is about taking a moment to see if you are one of those types of people who want to explore and discover your reason for being here on earth first and then go out in the world with clarity and empowerment to create something that puts your spirit and mind on fire. Ultimately, a life of meaning is what each person on earth wants. There are only some who do the upfront work to have it.

In chapter 4, we discuss being decisive. It is the quality that puts those who make their life and career a powerful and rewarding work of art to behold. This one quality cannot be side stepped. Without it, nothing would ever happen and forward movement would be only a wish. If we look at any leader who has changed lives, they all possessed the ability to be decisive.

Part of being decisive is the commitment to follow through on making your own life and career all that you want it to be. The actions to get there do not overwhelm the decisive person. Along with decisiveness, this person has focus and perseverance. It becomes impossible to fail when these qualities are in place. Deciding that you are in this to serve humanity using your unique gifts guarantees your success. The universe conspires to help this heart-felt request. Every time.

Chapter 5 is titled "Getting Out of Your Comfort Zone." Even though we all agree on this, many of us unknowingly fight and resist this when it comes down to it—even without realizing it. It is the very things that we avoid, discount, or lie to ourselves about that are the keys to our progress and success. Thinking we know better than what the universe wants us to understand is evidence that we do not.

It takes a fully honest person to step out of their comfort zone. This is what heroes, or heroines, are made of. It is our living version of a resurrection. Laying down the old self to allow the new one to be born. Or more accurately, allowing the true self to show her full and divine power

Chapter 6 is dedicated to the power of belief. Our lives mirror every belief we carry. Some are keepers and some sabotage our desired results. You will learn that just saying we believe something else doesn't work. Belief is not an intellectual matter. It is deep in the subconscious and wants to stay. Removing limiting beliefs and allowing the true ones to take place, eliminates a lot of wasted effort and frustration.

In chapter 7, you will see how innovation and perspective can outwit what you may deem as a limitation. When one becomes a problem solver, ceilings are broken.

I'm going to take a stab here. I bet that there are great and intense talents in you that either are just partially uncovered or are completely invisible to you today. How exciting is that? Think of what you can achieve with full access to these! Life can be a miracle when you make the intention to discover your gifts. Your gifts to your purpose may yet be revealed.

Chapter 8 covers the importance of finding your unique talents and then giving them away. For the pure in heart, the only point in having a talent is to be able give it away. There is little fulfillment in discovering our gifts to merely give ourselves an identity. There is another profound concept here. Just because you can do something, does not mean it is what you are supposed to be doing in your life. It does not mean that is your purpose.

Peace comes to those who are living in alignment to their purpose and sharing all they have selflessly.

In chapter 9, our sixth and final step is surrender. All of the aforementioned steps will not work if we are not in a humble estate of surrender. We will be diving into the servant's heart, how deep humility is vital to finding one's core truth of themselves. While this may be common knowledge, in true authentic practice, it is very rare to find and more difficult to achieve than one might suspect. However, we just start where we are and deepen the process. The more you surrender and let go in order to achieve a pure servant's heart with humility, the happier, more in tune, and joyful life becomes.

There is no limit. This process of surrender never stops giving. The more you are, the more you can give. The more you can give, the richer life becomes. The more you know yourself and other people, the better you can run and grow your business. You are in charge of how far you would like to go with this.

Clarity of Your Purpose

God is giving us so many clues to be able to discern lower- to higher-purpose activities and career choices. With enough space, desire, and willingness to see them, they become so obvious, we wonder how we ever could have missed it in the first place for so many years. It would be tremendously enlightening if we could see the world, and ourselves with that level of open spiritual clarity. What do you think would happen in your life if this were your experience?

I hope you take this opportunity of inward journey to find what you are looking for. The more of this work that you can do, the more closely you will be to your highest path. The secret is that in the becoming, we find the doing. We must become before we can do.

This book and this work are about gaining more clarity and fullness of self. Here we start to uncover your unique superpowers, find your dream career, and build the balanced and exhilarating life you are seeking. We will now dive into processes that my clients have used which produces results faster than was thought was possible.

Chapter 4

THE POWER OF DECISIVENESS AND PERSEVERANCE

"In order to answer the question
"Where am I going?" you must possess decisiveness"
—Sunday Adelaja

STEP 1: BE BOLD. BE DECISIVE. PERSEVERE.

One trait that all successful people share is their ability to make a decision. The second out there somewhere, but there was no visible evidence other than the birds. Carving their boats out of wood by hand, and with their own primitive source of navigation, they made the decision to find this mysterious land. trait common to them is their energy to persevere and follow through on making the decision a reality. You must first decide your course and then go about finding all the resources available to you to aid you in following through for the greatest and farthest-reaching chance for success.

The discovery of the Hawaiian Islands is one example of decision and perseverance that leaves one left with awe and inspiration. While no one knows the exact details of this historic and legendary feat, any part of it is worth telling.

How Determination and Perseverance Gave Birth to Hawaii

Some one thousand years ago, a group of brave and seafaring Polynesians began their exploration and habitation of the Hawaiian Islands. However, we need to back up four hundred years to about AD 600 and travel twenty-five hundred miles to how this began.

The inhabitants of the Marquesas Islands noticed a bird called the Golden Plover that, each year, migrated north out over the great expanse of ocean. They knew there must be land

Following the birds with simply their boats, paddles, and human strength, the brave explorers would row as fast as they could after the birds in hope of reaching this land. The birds were swifter at flying than the men were at paddling, so they would lose sight of the birds and have to turn back home, only having gone a short distance. Each year when the birds returned, using their navigation system, they would pick it up again where they left off. Each year, the Polynesians would gain small margins of ocean bit by bit, getting closer and closer to their goal of reaching these far-off islands.

Generation after generation for about four hundred years, they persevered to reach their destination. Four hundred years! Never quitting and never letting doubt overtake their resolve to conquer this dream, they finally won. Their decision to discover a new land became a reality.

To further put what they accomplished into modern perspective, it takes around thirty days to sail from the Marquesas Islands to the Hawaiian Islands with modern technology. After four hundred or so years, the concept of the Hawaiian Islands could have easily become a tall tale or mythical story told around a fire, thus dismissing the evidence of the birds as a magical play of the gods. However, it is obvious that these people were wise souls with great ambition and would not allow the impossible to cloud their vision. They revealed the genius inside them to make their firm decision to find the islands and persevered valiantly without wavering.

We all have this genius inside us. It is our duty to tap into it. We were designed with the advantage to succeed. You are nature's greatest miracle. Take a moment and breathe that in.

Feel, say, and believe that you are a masterpiece. You are an expression of God, of the universe. You are perfection becoming more and more complete each day. Do not put that thought down. Do not think that there is anything you cannot become, do, or achieve.

If you ever competed in a sport—did gymnastics, ballet or anything physical—then you know it takes some determination to do your best. Even a game of kick ball at recess can bring out the drive to run as fast as you can, even for a moment. Think of a time when you felt physically free. Feeling so excited to get to the swings that you thought your legs would not get you there fast enough. You were for a brief moment, laser-focused on one goal. There is a liberation with focus. Deciding what you want and persevering to actualize the goal is very empowering and inspiring for those who watch.

The people of the Marquesas Islands are an inspiration in what they accomplished. It is more than the discovery of an island; it is in the example of human potential that brings this story to still be told over one thousand years later. In this way, they hold their place in history.

Everything Holds Its Place

Everything in nature, each plant, animal, and rock has its place in this world. There is nothing in creation that is not important or beautiful. Have you ever had the experience of seeing a pet or a beautiful landscape and your heart swells? The dog and the landscape don't even know what they are doing. They are just being. They are just doing what they do best. This is just being a dog and being a landscape. There is no effort.

There is no feeling of "what if I fail at being this dog self that I am." It is impossible for the dog to fail. It is a dog being nothing but being true to himself. The tree in the landscape just stands there. Exuding her beauty day after day. She is constant and stalwart. There is no question of quitting being a tree. She just stands in her truth and gives selflessly to all who may admire her. We can all simplify our lives by making our decision to be our greatest selves inherent in all we do. Make the decision once to find your career and be resolved. In this way, we can learn from the dog and the landscape by retraining ourselves to get to our core. In the words of the early modern dance pioneers, "Be a tree."

How to Make Decision and Perseverance Easier

The dog, the tree, and the landscape all have another secret. They have a certain knowing that they are part of a greater whole. Without egos, they are not in the state of separation like we are. They can draw energy from everything around because they know they are not alone.

When someone makes the decision to be and serve at their best and for their purpose, standing in their truth like the tree, the universe conspires and moves mountains to make sure you are able to do so. With your decision, commitment, and perseverance to achieve your highest good, God and All That Is rallies around and through you.

Below, in "Home Plate," another creative story I wrote some years ago, look for decision, perseverance, and the boy's sense of connection to the universe and how that helped him draw up energy to realize his burning desire to make a home run. See where this has happened in your life or where you have observed someone outside yourself, whether you know them or not, who has achieved this in at least some aspect of their life.

Home Plate

Laser-focused, Mate pulled up all he had. He had been training for this game all year. At first, he wanted to win to show the world, particularly the bully who had been mocking him for years, that he was capable. But that feels like an insignificant reason now. As he ran, he knew he was larger than that.

Racing, his feet were like lightening, his heart and lungs burned, and he could barely see through the dust and sweat. He wasn't sure he was even running in a straight line to hit the next base, but he had to push his body to keep up with his spirit; there was no time to think.

As he closed in on third base, Mate could no longer feel himself in his body. It was as if he were bursting out of his flesh, and his legs were dutiful to the cause. His feet and the ground were obeying his will, and he had energy like he had ever known before. It was no longer about the game or anyone else. It was now just him connecting to this unseen power. Like a trillion atomic particles all firing at once. He could feel the passion of a thousand men surge through his body, but at the same time it was only him and his will.

Flashing into his mind with no warning, he felt as if he were in the jungle. He saw he was one with a hungry tiger chasing the only prey in sight for days. Every muscle, every nerve ending was working in unison—firing and exploding, summoning the same power used to create new galaxies. The tree branches, the fallen logs, the thick leaves, the dense air were all there to support the hunt. His huge paws expanded with every step, cracking small twigs and breaking a weakened, mossy hollow log. The tiger's claws dug into the ground and kicked back the warm, soft earth in a hypnotic rhythm. The receptive soil allowed the imprint of his paw to leave its commanding mark.

With his entire body responding viscerally to the echoes of the past, his hind legs sprang forward with surety and purpose—his purpose. It smelled of the millions of years of rich, organic matter working together as one—earthy and tangible denseness filling his nostrils with every powerful breath. He could sense the bodies of countless creatures and plant life left behind to nurture the soil given as a precious gift. All coming together in a knowing-ness for this hunt, for this moment.

The noise became louder as Mate rounded third base. Chants of encouragement came as loudly as the silence of those resisting his win. There was for this moment, no past, no future. There is only now, the home plate in front of him and his peace in knowing all was as it should be. His intention to win became a reality even before he crossed the plate, but somehow that was no longer the goal. It was then that he found alignment—the moment of unwavering decision—or rather, a knowing by connecting to what is.

You Have Support

In the story above, Mate began with an intention, he made the decision to make a home run. In the process of being fully present in the now and taking fearless action, he was able to effortlessly connect himself to God and to all of creation. This gave him intense energy and support. It was as if all of creation that ever existed was rounding third base to the home plate with him. He forgot himself, he put down his ego and allowed himself to succeed. Mate's intense, yet edifying run is a metaphor for the support that is possible for us on a larger life scale.

There Is Always a Way

Remember our Polynesian friends earlier? They saw a greater cause in gaining the land. This was not just for fun for a vacation spot. The terrain in the Marquesas Islands was forbidding and unfriendly. They wanted more as a people. The brave ones who risked their lives to cross an untamed ocean did it for the love of their families and communities. They pooled their energy together for centuries and finally won the land for which they hoped. With all of that effort, it only made sense that they first believed they could do it. True decision, like Mate and the Polynesians had, is knowing the win before it happens, because you will ensure it.

Make the Decision

Decisive people are people who make a difference in their lives. Living in indecision will take you on a wild goose chase. It's letting circumstance rule. Compelling excuses dominate the indecisive individual's mantra. Decision is being mindful and even diplomatically and graciously saying no to the things that would interfere with the larger vision.

Every great person has been able to accomplish what they knew was theirs by decision and perseverance. There is no question about whether this thing will happen for them or not. It is already done. There is just the time it takes for the doing and the personal growth needed to catch up to the vision. And I promise, if you decide and start today, it will not take you four hundred years.

An indispensable part of holding a vision is to start living it now in what capacity you can. The vision is one thing, the action from a willing heart is the great power that fulfills dreams. Start with what you can do now, in daily life. Use what you have and bless other's lives today. It will seem like such a small thing, and you will wonder what impact you are having. However, it will create a ripple effect that you will see at some point in your life. You will be able to do many more great new things now.

Chapter 5

THE WISDOM TO STEP OUTSIDE YOUR COMFORT ZONE

*"Life always begins with one step
outside of your comfort zone."*
—Shannon L. Alder

STEP 2: HAVING THE WISDOM TO STEP OUTSIDE YOUR COMFORT ZONE

This brings us to our second step to discovering your purpose and creating that perfect and magical career you are envisioning. It is the willingness and foresight to be a little, or a great deal, uncomfortable; in some instances, that marks a true disciple of transformation. The further you want to go in your life, the more you will see that being uncomfortable is a perpetual requirement for the genuine self-improvement needed to reach new heights.

For those of you who want to "go big or go home", the universe will respond in a very loving way to give you exactly what it is you need to become in order for you to manifest the greater and more rewarding things you are seeking. It is an insightful and mature person who allows discomfort to become a welcomed friend when it arises, because it means there is something wonderful happening.

Feeling uncomfortable in the midst of something new is the way we know we have an area to be healed, matured, and strengthened. It tells us where we next need to grow and reveals the next layer of the metaphorical onion to be peeled away. Any resistance to the process of transcending fears, even at the slightest level, will slow down or, if held indefinitely, will sabotage your best of intentions if you do not learn to recognize the discomfort for the merciful gift that it is.

Although it is not usually intentional, resistance goes largely unnoticed by the person doing the resisting. We can craft very articulate and convincing reasons for staying in resistance to the change our deepest and wisest self knows we are ready for. It is a very human response to resist change and upward movement.

Even when logically one would say she does not want problem X, often declaring it out loud to convince others and herself of her desire to be past problem X, it is not uncommon for her to fabricate a reason to stay in the current problem, because at least it is known to her.

It's not your fault when resistance first shows itself in any given issue. It is the old self not wanting to die, or equally said, it is the current ego wanting to stay in charge. Metaphorically, you could think of the old self, or current ego, as a bouncer with strict orders to not let anyone with new ideas or fresh ambitions enter the party. With help and personal determination, you can have the ability to override your old self fairly quickly and discard the ways she is no longer serving you.

Lack of Pain versus Pleasure

The old self when challenged, will often begin to argue and find evidence for staying where she is, even when she just was complaining about how hard things are a few minutes ago. The viable solution to a problem could be presented and handed on a silver platter, and the old self, if allowed, will work to find every flaw in the solution and turn the story around that she in fact does not struggle with that thing she was just before admitting. That is the old self being so desperate to stay, that she confuses having less pain with having true joy. Shaving off pain is not the same thing as having pleasure.

Fear of the Unknown

There are many things happening on a spiritual level with resistance to leaving your comfort zone that is too complex to address here. But, in essence, it is the fact that we fear the unknown. Fear of the unknown will make us uncomfortable and cause us to want to go back to what we know, because it feels safe and seemed to work for us in a prior circumstance. We know how to do A, B, and C and can predict the results each time. However, this uncharted territory of X, Y, and Z, feels like a hazardous enigma.

Resistance will come up and rear its head at often unexpected times. But in making our goals more important than our fears, we find the solution to transcend resistance and make positive change. Some fears are very deep and need much more work than a simple decision to overcome them. They can be deeply rooted in our history. However, if your dream is more important to you than the temporary discomfort to heal a limitation, you will be led to the competent help you need to permanently be rid of it, and not take a lifetime to do it. We stop feeding it once we decide to heal it. With our fears healed, we become much more effective and can be consistently bold in taking those steps required to achieve our goals.

The good news is, as mentioned above, the need to stay in the known as the only safe place to be can be overcome. We show that bouncer that having a new idea can be a very welcome benefit to the old, stale party, and he will retire his position. The human spirit has the capability to move out of fear and into love and hope, which is where we thrive.

Fear Is an Illusion

In fact, fear is a temporary and illusionary human condition and is not natural to our true selves. The late French philosopher Pierre Teilhard de Chardin put this very well when he said, "We are not human beings having a spiritual experience. We are spiritual beings having a human experience." Thus we are here, in part, to overcome the illusion of fear.

Once we make the unwavering decision to do the internal work to become what is needed for the life we want to create, we are, in turn, declaring our willingness to trust the process of growth that comes with allowing ourselves to face uncomfortable things. Thus, welcoming and being grateful for some discomfort affords us the opportunity to make a new life happen.

• • • • •

"The Dot and the Speck," my short and fun poem (transformation should still be fun!), allows us to see clearly on which side of the fence we want to be. Deep inside, at our core, all human beings want to be the "dot," as you will see. Those who are willing to commit to stretching themselves are the dots-in-action. Freedom, peace, and empowerment are at the end of the path for a self-declared and in-action dot. Those who feel this level of freedom, peace, and empowerment are the ones who enjoy the mysteries and rewards that life has to offer.

The Dot and the Speck

Way far off in Yala-kazot,
there was a small circle, and inside, a dot.
The dot danced around, but soon she felt bored
with nothing to conquer, and nothing explored.

With all of her courage and all of her might
she pushed out the circle, no matter the fight.
The circle grew larger and more exciting each day.
The fresh air made her strong and happy to play.

But, way far off in Yala-kazeck
there was a small circle, and inside, a speck.
The speck danced around but never saw more.
She was content to never explore.

She stayed in her cramped circle and never looked out.
Never was curious what the world was about.
Her muscles grew weak and the circle stayed small.
The air became stale, she found no joy at all.

So what can we learn from the dot and the speck
from Yala-kazot and Yala-kazeck?
See, if we stay in our comfort zone and never go stretch.
We will die an old grumpy, or even a wretch.

But if we take courage and seek for more life,
Expand our circle and push through the strife.
We find joy in our mind, our soul, and our heart.
Each breath is a blessing, and each day, a new start!

_____

Life Is Worth the Investment

Nothing of true and eternal value comes for free. And it is the very process of feeling uncomfortable and transcending the fear that prepares you for the bigger things you will embark on. There are no shortcuts or going around it. A shortcut might give one temporary relief, but the issue will eventually resurface until it is completely dealt with. We must go through to get to the other side.

To say your life is worth the investment is an understatement. The person who can forsake and heal their fear-laden "speck" areas and embrace the "dot" lifestyle are the ones who become free. This is where we hop off the slower-moving trolley and onto a speed train to our success.

Chapter 6
WE FIND WHAT
WE BELIEVE IN

"Sometimes the heart sees what is invisible to the eye."
—H. Jackson Brown, Jr.

STEP 3: ALIGN THE BELIEF OF YOURSELF TO MATCH YOUR FULL POTENTIAL

How we see ourselves at the deepest subconscious level is how we show up in the world. The power of belief is something we hear about repeatedly. It is in quotes, articles, books, speeches, and movies. However, the influence that belief has in every manifestation of your life cannot be overstated. The power of belief is the source that drives our relationships, views, actions, and the results in our life. In this chapter, you will learn how changing limiting beliefs is vital to increase success and fulfillment.

We Have to Be Open to Seeing It

The work I do with my clients raises one to a higher perspective, increases one's capacity to love, increases intuition, decreases judgment, and decreases fear to name a few of the powerful elements gained in true transformation. These attributes connect you to having what you need in life to succeed and to your internal power to fulfill all of your dreams and ambitions. This transformation is like a rebirth.

I appreciate the butterfly and what she teaches us about ourselves and our life path. She symbolizes rebirth, beauty and great transformation.

Transformation to Butterfly

Think of the innocent little caterpillar crawling along. She is only knowing herself as a caterpillar. Day in and day out, living her caterpillar life. If you told the caterpillar she would someday be this completely different creature, with colorful wings that flew, she would stare in disbelief. By looking down at her caterpillar body, she sees only little legs and a furry torso, proving and supporting her belief that she is definitely a caterpillar. From her perspective, she sees only branches and leaves and what they have to offer her. Having wings and access to the vastness of the sky and the opportunity there is not yet in her paradigm. The knowledge and vision of her full potential is not yet available to her.

Luckily, nature does not give the caterpillar a choice but to evolve into her full potential. She is induced into a major metamorphosis, her DNA guides the process, and she miraculously transforms. She has a chrysalis opportunity, I like to call it. The opportunity to release the old paradigms and emerge more empowered as the new and glorious version of self. Our chrysalis moments in life can be compared to when we face ourselves and are willing to let go of what is no longer serving us to embrace the new.

I think it is no accident that Mother Nature has provided us with this example of complete transformation as a parallel to the spiritual evolution of the human race. Those who can believe that they have a potential beyond what they can now see or conceive, and make the choice to do the work, are the ones who get to find out how rich that potential really is.

Unlike the obliged caterpillar, if we want to make larger evolutionary changes in our lives, we must make the choice to do so. We cannot take a long nap and wake up brand new (darn it!). But honestly, in our wisdom, we would not want an authorized or dictated life. The magic of self-discovery is the freedom to choose to seek our own power. Just like it is in the grand design of the caterpillar DNA to change herself to butterfly, it is in our spiritual structure to transform into higher-functioning versions of ourselves.

With the discovery of the sky, the butterfly has a much higher view. She has access to more of the world, its information and can increase her connection to it. As we continue to improve ourselves, we gain access to much more wisdom and truth that was not before available to us. It was not available before because we did not know this level of enlightenment even existed. So, we did not know to seek it.

In addition to flight in the sky, she is attracted to flowers, puppies and many more inspiring things, because vibration is elevated. We are attracted to things that match our vibration. Being curious to know what new heightened "butterfly world" is available to you is both an adventurous and honorable idea. It is an indication that there is belief inside that the new world is attainable.

Belief Dictates the Outward Result

The work I do with clients always circles back to improving their belief system of how they see themselves, how they communicate and relate to God and how they see the world. Without belief in something, no amount of doing can permanently change the current circumstance. The belief will always dictate the end result. You can learn skills and systems, tell yourself you can do it, and work all day, but without the belief that the goal belongs to you, you will feel like you are climbing uphill on a mountain of loose gravel trying to do it. Either your health and well-being will suffer, or you will quit to save yourself.

If, for example, a client, by process of working with me to further her dream career, discovers that running seminars is the next macro step in growing her business, the work is not the logistics of how to set up a successful seminar; that's fairly easy. The work is in how she believes that she can succeed at it. If she has a fear that no one will come, then we work through the source of that false belief, which is never as straightforward as one may think. We are complex creatures. Once all the layers of that fear are systematically healed, the false belief is organically replaced by the truth.

If a client declares he wants to know how to be directed by God on a deeper personal level, but he has a false belief deep inside that he is not good enough to have that level of direction, by simply sitting there and listening for what God has for him will not work unless he can believe the truth that he is of worth to receive more communication from God. We heal the misconception. The truth is, we always are. As we grow and open spiritually, more and more becomes available for us to recognize, see and hear.

Believe There Is a Sky Available

If all anyone had to do was declare what they wanted that is good, there would be no poverty, no pain, no loneliness. However, as we all know, it doesn't work that way. We must be willing to do the internal work to improve ourselves so we can in turn improve our surrounding circumstances. That takes time. Without the belief that the personal improvement desired is available to us, or that there is indeed a sky there, although invisible to us, just waiting to be discovered, we will get impatient and stop, do a little work and turn away, or not make any attempts.

It is our deep subconscious beliefs that mold our self-image, our personal circumstance, and as a collective human race, the circumstance of the world at large. You are how you see yourself. You see others and the world as positioned, or through the lens of how you see yourself. We will only realize there is a sky available if we can believe in the vision of our own butterfly potential. Everything is a mirror of your deep internal beliefs about your own identity.

We Find What We Are Looking For

We find what we believe in and are looking for. If we are looking for the beauty inside ourselves and in others, then we will have breathless moments at the most simple of things. Allowing our heart to lead honestly, without tainted filters or underground agendas, we find the greatest of treasures. This includes being able to see in yourself where your greatest talents and contributions are inside.

I had an experience with a client a few years ago that led me to write this next short story coming up, "Finding Pennies." He was searching to unlock the phenomena of what we create verses what is provided. Look for when you may have had something similar come up in your life. What was your conclusion?

Finding Pennies

A friend, speaking of his personal journey, said how at one earlier point in his life and now again, he is always finding pennies. Pennies are in his path constantly.

Was it weird luck, superstition, or the universe trying to tell him something? I wondered…

Very interestingly, following our conversation, I started seeing pennies everywhere!

We both mused on the situation. Were angels putting pennies in our way? Coincidence?

I went to prayer and meditation on the seemingly small, but significant mysterious penny findings.

My answer that came to me was that the pennies are always there, but we are now finding them because we have become open to finding them.

Aha! You find what you look for and believe in.

And the grander lesson:

We all possess everything we need to succeed inside of us.

It is already there; we just have to be open to seeing it!

Our light, our unique gifts can shine as easily and effortlessly as my friend and I find and pick up pennies.

———————————————

Chapter 7

OUTSMARTING LIMITATION

*"Your only limitation is the
one you set up in your own mind."*
—Napoleon Hill

STEP 4: INNOVATION OVER LIMITATION

What happens when you put an ant on a piece of clean paper? The little guy just crawls wherever he wants to go. Now, put the ant in the center of the paper and draw a circle around the ant with a black marker. What happens now? If you have ever seen this, it is both entertaining and very telling. Instead of wandering around with freedom to explore his full sheet of paper and beyond, the ant stays within the confines of the circle as if he is bumping up against a wall.

Albert Einstein did much of his work through meditation and having visionary experiences. He let his mind see past the limits, then went to work to prove it after the fact. He allowed what others could not see past to come to him and hence became the father of modern physics. The Wright brothers, Thomas Edison, Christopher Columbus, and, one of my favorites, Galileo (who was centuries ahead of his time) achieved their contributions to the world by ignoring others' limitations.

Breaking Past the Illusion of Limitations

Eighty-four yoga poses in a two hour, very regimented class in a 106-degree room with 30 percent humidity. You really have the opportunity to step up your limited thinking in there. Taught by a loving and goal-oriented world champion, the class offered limitless opportunities to improve. Although the physical aspect of the class is very demanding, the much larger piece is mental and spiritual endurance. As I was a newbie in a class full of award-winning competitors, I stood out like a sore thumb.

For strengthening and endurance, we are required (OK, encouraged) to hold plank for three minutes starting up on our hands and then moving down to our forearms for another three minutes. At first, I was only making it a small portion, resting, and then getting back into it and feeling the suffering. Then my caring and experienced instructor said to hold it past the mind wanting to quit; hold it until your body just collapses. That is your real limit.

I was so excited to do this technique! You mean I can actually hold plank much longer? Empowered, I got into plank, let my mind take a back seat and just held it. The moment my body just gave out was a moment of pure joy. I had found my real limit! And guess what? Plank, while still challenging, has never been more satisfying. I am holding it much longer and am less tired. Holding plank for a long time was not the problem, it was the mental drama that made it hard and imposed an untrue limitation.

The Mental Drama of Limitation

A wise coach framed the concept of limitation so well when she said that 20 percent of your success is knowing what to do and the other 80 percent is knowing how to manage the drama. We all create stories of why something is unavailable to us, and while we are doing that, they seem so real at the time. I want to introduce the remarkable woman Aimie Mullins, who not only saw past her limitation but also brilliantly turned it into her greatest asset.

Aimie Mullins Surpassing Limitations

Born without shin bones, Aimie had her legs amputated at the knee at one year of age, just as her peers were beginning to toddle around. Sometimes not included at school, she kept her spirits up by working hard in her classes and in softball and skiing, using wooden legs. In high school, Aimie, not wanting to be defined by her lack of lower limbs, reluctantly enrolled in an alternative meet with other amputees. To her astonishment, the other competitors had high tech, shock absorbent metal legs and most had one full normal leg. She didn't know these advancements existed. Running on her two old-fashioned wooden legs, she pushed herself even harder and ended up breaking a national record.

She next entered the long jump, a competition which double amputees are not "supposed" to enter. In a year, she broke the world record. Aimie went on to set records in the Paralympic Games in Atlanta in 1996, despite a setback when her prosthetic slipped off in one event. The following year she was named USA Track and Field's Disabled Athlete of the Year, and the National Association of Women in Education's 1997 Woman of Distinction.

With determination and interest in other fields outside of athletics, Aimie enrolled at Georgetown University; she was also selected for the prestigious Foreign Affairs internship program. She was the only woman among 250 men and, at age seventeen, the youngest person to work at the Pentagon in an internship. She graduated in 1998 from Georgetown's School of Foreign Service with a double major in history and diplomacy.

Aimie was also a model for L'Oreal and did runway with wooden boots made to look like real boots. Some applauded this innovation while others criticized it. At first, Aimie had legs made to look like regular human legs, to try to fit in; then she got inspired.

How Aimie Turned a Limitation into a Greater Strength

At first, Aimie had prosthetic legs made to look like regular human legs. Then she had a paradigm shift on how she viewed the social dynamic of her missing lower legs. She decided to break the norm of expectation and think in a new way. Those of us with full legs do not have the choice of how our legs appear; however, she had more creative license. She began to make legs that were works of art: twisty silicon, pointed darts, and even cheetah legs. This gave her the flexibility to be cast in films where other full-bodied actresses could not go.

Have you ever thought it would be fun to adjust your height for different situations? Well, Aimee can. She has prosthetics made at various lengths so she can be her birth height of 5'8" or taller on the days she feels like it. One of her friends commented, "Well, that's not fair!" That turns around the perspective for sure! Aimie found a way to make her own limitation her inspiration.

I wrote this next poem out of inspiration for Aimie and what she teaches us. She is now an energetic public speaker recognized for her dedication to helping children grow up with a mind open to breaking boundaries instead of creating them, like our little friend the ant on the paper.

 From Limitation to Inspiration, a Poem

There once lived a shoemaker, humble and neat.
Each day this elf created shoes, for needy feet.
Each day he reached for the leather and glue.
Each day he made shoes and nothing was new.

A sweet tiny elf breezed in, magnificent and bright.
She possessed an honest heart that produced its own light,
She had this beauty, this feature, this truly inspiring mark.
However, she donned no feet… and the difference was
  stark.

She had stubs that stopped where elves' feet otherwise go,
Born with no heels, no arches, no soles, not one toe.
She asked the cobbler to fashion beautiful tall boots,
So she could feign feet as her own attribute.
So the cobbler reached for the leather and glue.
He made the same boots that he already knew.
Like everyone else now, she matched *their* stride.
She greeted the world in ego and false pride.

She no longer flew and her wings forgot flight.
They no longer shone with their natural light.
She could no longer soar high and go up to see
the private creation of her true destiny.

She stayed in the fog, way down below
where the people with feet had little choice but to go.
Looking down, she ho-hummed as she saw her false feet.

She saw her limp wings and felt lifeless and beat.

She had a sudden spark—a whimsy, a thought.

She discovered how to be the Authentic Self she sought.

She asked the cobbler to *create* some wings.

He did—and they were marvelous things.

So now instead of boots and the mirage to conform

She has two sets of wings, very opposite the norm…

See, she put on wings where before she tried boots.

She ACCENTED HER GIFTS, her God-given loot.

She is the ONLY ONE with wings and the freedom to
    plan,

She tried springs and jets, as with the absence of feet—
    SHE CAN!

Stubs are her fate, her purpose, her chance

to shine her TRUE LIGHT, and dance her own dance.

Our Limitations Can Reveal Our Strengths

So not only are our limitations false barriers that can be broken, they can be disguised as our greatest asset. Our limitations can cause us to think more creatively.

Our true strengths are just crying out to be found, to be uncovered. The little elf here in this poem, at first got caught up in trying to fix her seeming limitation. She tried to be like everyone else. Finding herself very miserable, at the bottom, is what forced her create a new way.

The moment she saw that she should not be trying to fix what she thought was her weakness but to allow it to help her uncover her true strength was when she found this great capacity in her to fly. She has a life on purpose.

Answering the Call to Our Greatness

We all carry this story inside of us. At our core, there is a limitation of some kind to let go of. In my observation with clients, I notice that some people are not even aware of what their limitation is because it is not obvious. Hidden deep in there, are undiscovered mental and spiritual blocks, which take some exploring to find and are difficult to get through alone. If a limitation or limiting belief it is not obvious, not found and not transcended, one runs the risk of never learning their true strength.

If the elf had only feet like everyone else, she never, or most probably, would not have found that she could fly. Having feet could possibly have handicapped her in the end. Blessed is the one who desires go around and beyond their limitations. Life starts to look lucky for those folks.

Finding Clues

One way to start the discovery is to see what has followed you. What I mean by that is what are comments you have gotten along the way in your life, including in childhood, that are clues as to what is your real gift. Looking back, I clearly now see that since I was very young, I was told that I am very patient. As I grew a little older, say high school, I started seeing that others, even strangers would like to tell me of their inward thoughts and feelings and seek the comfort of someone who would listen without judgment. My husband would watch as a stranger at a mall or the cashier at a restaurant would end up confiding and even crying with what is going on in their lives. It baffled him.

There were several other things that followed me along these lines. In hindsight I see as the clues that were hidden to me for my purpose as a healer, mentor and intuitive. You have these clues too. They will look subtle and seem like little and insignificant things, but they are actually great clues. Trust it. What can be difficult is how to sort through and put these clues to work in an actual career. Alone this can be difficult and take many years to find it. My work shaves years off the process.

The other clue is it will not feel like work. Yes, it can be hard at times to figure out the next step or what have you to do, but the work at large, will be motivating and feel supportive of your health, happiness, and well-being. When in your true talents, you will feel motivation to do it and to give it your all because it gives to you. It feeds your spirit. Your value in the world is priceless. You are worth all the effort to get to this place in your life.

Chapter 8

DISCOVER YOUR TALENTS THAT DEFINE YOUR PURPOSE, THEN GIVE THEM AWAY

*"True happiness involves the
full use of one's power and talents."*
—**John W. Gardner**

STEP 5: FOCUS YOUR TALENTS AND GIVE THEM AWAY

Pure bliss in life is to find your specific unique talents and then give them away. Ultimately, this benefits you, your family, and humanity. Having the desire to know who you are and what you can contribute to the world is you in perfection. There are many examples of people who have understood this principle. Let's look at Mother Theresa. Her mission was to help lift those in poverty and distress. Marie Curie's contribution in chemistry and physics propelled the sciences light-years ahead. Grace Hopper created one of the first easy-to-use computer languages, greatly advancing computer programming.

These women did not stumble across their contributions. It started with the desire to fully use what they had to contribute. They gave what they had without reservation. And they gave what they had with focus to help uplift others as their end result. It was their focus to concentrate their efforts on their talents with the most impact.

When you choose a career of purpose, you will lose what you do not want and gain all that you do want, and much, much more. Once you make an intention and work for what is aligned with your purpose, the universe conspires with you to make sure it happens. This is what greatness is made of. The world needs you–exactly you. Authentically you.

The Talent with the Most Purpose Wins

We all have more than one talent. The final destination is to eventually find which talents are actually for your purpose, meaning which talents you need to put energy into and develop because it serves your highest purpose. Finding your purpose is what the universe is asking of you. In order to answer this call, it will be necessary for you to put some things down or to the side. You are gifted person. You can do whatever it is you want to do. Some things come very easily. You can see that with focus, you could have a level of success there. But is it in the highest wisdom for you to pursue? We live in a world with a massive amount of opportunity. There is more opportunity now than there ever has been and that is growing each day.

This makes it even more difficult for you to narrow down your specific direction to follow. Let's add it up. You are a talented and intelligent woman, you have access to whatever it is you would want to learn and develop, and the world offers opportunity for anything you can throw at it. It would be much easier if you did not have so many options. Soon though, the easy, limited options turn to frustration and a will to break free.

Miracles occur when a person is disciplined and focused on their gifts specific to their purpose and then gets out there and shares them with the world. When you add in that you have the intention to love others and help them in your unique way, you become an unbeatable force.

Trust You Will Be Supported

It can be kind of scary to trust enough to set down and leave behind something you can do well, but it is only scary without the fuller vision. When you can trust that the universe will always support those who are honestly seeking to serve in their greatest capacity, moving forward into a new arena, maybe even an unknown arena becomes an exciting adventure and a welcomed blessing. Discovering your talent with the most impact is key.

If It's Not for Your Purpose, It's Not Yours

It is quite common for someone who has found a level of success to hear them say that they searched and dedicated themselves to one area for a time solely because they were capable of doing it. Then they come to the conclusion, after years of moderate success, that it was not their purpose. Going down a secondary trail did not allow a fullness of expression and satisfaction.

If you are searching for the most fulfilling, gratifying, and meaningful career, it requires the soul searching and personal work of those with a strong conviction and motivated continence. We only have so much time and energy in a lifetime. Making your investment in yourself count in a definitive way is clarity of life on steroids.

Allow the next person take the multitude of secondary talents you could develop, as it may be primary for them in their purpose. It is your job to find your primary gifts, focus, and expand them and, like Mother Theresa, Marie Curie, and Grace Hopper, freely give that gift to others in your greatest capacity.

The story below, "The Harp and the Frogs," demonstrates two very different outlooks and approaches to life. The first one, symbolized by the princess in a tower consumed by herself and away from the world, is a passive and entitled mindset. Consider how the princess is waiting for something to rescue her by finding her fake solution (collecting frogs), in order to have the desired outcome (the prince), and turned inward instead of thinking how she can help others. That magic-bullet mindset instead drove away her desired outcome and left her still stuck with little.

Conversely, the second heartening example, represented by the peasant girl validates the power of a servant's heart. She looks for a way to give to others, invests herself in the cause, and attracts more than she could hope for into her life. This approach to life is the most simple, fruitful, gratifying, and peaceful. It creates a compounding effect. One good thing builds the foundation for the next to take its position.

 **The Harp and the Frogs**

All she did was wait.

A little snoozy in the head, the princess dallied high in the top room of her moth-eaten castle.

Living in the future and too timid to seize the day, the princess waited and wondered when she would be rescued from her pity and the staleness of her life and find a frog, any frog, that would turn into a prince.

The problem with waiting for a frog to turn into a prince is it seemed to take a really long time. And another thing she thought—what if this prince promised no more than a mild improvement.

With nothing to lose and hope for anything to gain, she thought of a plan to speed things up and to have a better chance for a happy or at least an adequate life.

The princess began collecting frogs. Many, many, many frogs.

Fat ones, small ones, green ones with spots, brown ones with no spots.

Some had really buggy eyes, some had big chins, and some had silly toes.

It didn't matter to her, because surely one would work out splendidly.

Now, there was a beautiful peasant girl with a smile that shone like diamonds that lived down in the village. Unspoiled and keen, she had a different idea.

She wanted to play the harp and inspire all the people of the village to be happy with her beautiful music.

One problem though: she did not have a harp.

So she devised a savvy plan.

Every day, she would go to the harp maker's shop and dust and sweep the floor.

Each day she cleaned, the harp maker would put a small coin in a jar.

And when the jar was full, he would make a lovely harp just for her.

Meanwhile, the princess was still going about collecting frogs. It was getting rather noisy in her chambers with all of the incessant croaking.

A real live Prince rode by and wondered what all the terrible noise was about. Bewildered and even somewhat repulsed, he rode away to get farther from the ruddy sounds.

Now the day came when the jar was full of coins. The peasant girl had swept the floor exactly 624 times, never missing a day.

She joyfully received her lovely harp to play to inspire others to be happier.

A real live prince rode by and heard the beautiful music. Feeling happier for hearing the sounds, he followed the music and saw the peasant girl playing.

He married the peasant girl, and she played in many more lands, inspiring more and more people to feel joy and pursue their dreams.

The princess? Well, needless to say she is still alone, waiting with her loathsome expectations, not willing to give, not willing to open her heart or take a risk. Blinded by her own fear, she waits in her musty room full of noisy, warty, bug-eyed frogs.

So the moral of the story?

Turning in turns all away.

Giving away brings all in.

_____

Your Truth

Develop and search fervently for your talents, sacrifice for it, and give it away selflessly. What is the symbolism of the prince here? The prince is the peace that comes with finding and utilizing your gifts. It is being on the road to fulfilling your life's purpose. There is no substitute to finding this peace. It is not fleeting and can withstand and support you greatly through any of life's challenges. Continuous and safe, being aligned with your purpose is the secret to a rich and happy life. Your prince will find you, or rather, you are allowing him, the peace, to come to you.

Be Grateful for the Present Moment

Where have you seen people in the world like the princess in the tower? One mark of princess behavior is not living in the present moment and living only in the future. When you can be at peace with today, this very moment, you are tapping into your true self. Being present and grateful for today actually makes creating the future as you would like it to develop. You then can have great power in your actions because there is more clarity about where to take action.

Our Truth Stands under the Surface

The princess didn't want to do her internal work. She was too busy and distracted collecting frogs in the hope that one would turn into a prince. Collecting frogs is a metaphor for chasing busy work in order to stay in denial. It was a way to remain stagnant in her life. She hoped that she would be rescued from her own work and evolution so that she could set up a cozy, false reality to save her some temporary discomfort. In doing this, she is actually augmenting the discomfort and protracting the inevitable. There is no way to wish away or escape yourself in this way. And the secret is it is much, much easier to just take care of it than to let it linger, keep bothering you and sabotaging your life. My champion clients know this secret. They take a little time with me and get it done.

Your truth stands underneath the surface and does not go away. She missed the prince, her opportunity to express her purpose, and he did not even see her. He was even repulsed by what she was doing.

The peasant girl got the larger picture. She began with a desire to serve others, and started with what called to her, the harp. Not yet possessing the harp, nor having a quick method in front of her, she found a way to obtain it. Her time in the shop is a metaphor for the internal preparation we must go through to be the person who can serve in a higher capacity. She was willing to pay her dues. Failure or rejection was possible, but she wanted to serve more than she was worried about herself. It offered her the opportunity to fulfill her purpose and draw the prince (peace) to her. It was all about her genuine action and willingness to work for what she believed in without fear or worry about what it might look like to others.

The Genius in Playing Big

This was not discussed in the story, but I'm sure there would be some who would disapprove of her choice to work like that to buy a harp and play it for anyone who wanted to hear. Maybe her father thought she should be going to school or her mother wanted her to follow in her own footsteps in something else. Maybe there were outright harp-haters in her village and around the land. When one is living in their truth, there will always be opposition. It will ruffle someone's feathers.

It is easier to play small, not make too big a splash, as to never offend a soul. The occasional other person will not like it when someone is being bold and living their truth. It causes them to see something in themselves that they do not want to see. You can always find a reason why not playing big is the right choice, and that will always come down to a fear of some kind, often fear of being seen or judged. In fact, if you do not have any push back from anyone, then you are not reaching far enough in yourself to really use your talents and purpose here on earth. An authentic life is the pebble thrown in the water.

The Ripple Effect

It actually serves others in such a greater way if you are true to yourself. Firstly, you reach those who are waiting for you. Those who will have their lives changed for the better in great ways because of your courage to step forward in your power. Secondly, it gives those who are wanting to step out the encouragement to do it themselves. This creates a ripple effect like none other. It causes people several steps away from your contact to be profoundly affected in positive ways just by your choice to move on with your truth.

Lastly, it causes those who may be against you a chance to learn and grow themselves. Some may make the choice to see your courage in a new way. Those people now see the truth of their own fear behind their initial discrimination. In taking an about-face, they start throwing their pebbles in the water and become huge influencers themselves—ripple after ripple after ripple.

You Are Meant to Do Great Things

Nelson Mandela, as well as many other great spiritual teachers, once said, "Your playing small does not serve the world. Who are you not to be great?" Yes, you are meant to be great and do great things. Find your harp and be awesome.

Chapter 9

THE SECRET
OF SURRENDER

*"The greatness of a man's power
is the measure of his surrender."*

—William Booth

STEP 6: SURRENDER TO YOUR HIGHER PURPOSE

Surrender is the secret that everyone who has made a lasting impact on the world knows and lives by. These people are genuine. Some have lived quiet lives and only those whom they knew will ever know of what they did. Others are written in the annals of history. However it may look on the outside, their impact on others is tremendous. When you come from a true and authentic place of being teachable and humble, what you want becomes in alignment with your purpose. Life becomes a beautiful and exciting masterpiece. In our previous discussions around decisiveness, making space, overcoming our limitations, giving away our talents, and having the courage to go outside of our comfort zone, these efforts will be blighted without the existence of surrender, humility, and a teachable heart. Surrendering to the concept that we do not know everything and surrendering our egos is the necessary step to self-advancement. If you are serious about taking this wonderful adventure in this phase of your life, and you want it to mean something and be on fire with your purpose, make doing so in surrender your priority.

Surrender Is Ever-Deepening

Surrendering is an ever-deepening process. Once I find a new level of surrender, another one appears. Humility asks us to acknowledge our shortcomings. It requires that we admit when we are holding onto ego, and then letting go of it. If you have an arrogance in an area, then you are not alone. It is a very human vice. Few people recognize their own areas of arrogance, because it would require one to acknowledge it and do the work to take the bitter cup. "Humility is the first of the virtues," Oliver Wendell Holmes Jr. jestingly said, "for other people."

Benjamin Franklin, at age twenty-seven, frustrated by his unproductive circumstance, wisely made a list of twelve attitudes and actions for his own improvement. He once asked a friend to look over his list. What his friend told him probably stung a little. Franklin wrote in his autobiography that the man "kindly informed me that I was generally thought proud; that my pride showed itself frequently in conversation." Humility was to be the thirteenth virtue in his project.

That story is so encouraging because it demonstrates a level of surrender consciously sought by those who make a big difference in the world. It would be curious to see how history would have been written if Franklin would not have gone to work on himself like that. Perhaps we would not know his name or have his contributions.

Discovering Your Purpose Is Found in the Surrender

Behind the smoke screen of presumptions, and it can be extremely subtle, is a wall to keep our fragile areas protected. These fragile areas of us are in fear. We fear knowing what might happen if we allow ourselves to show vulnerably. The secret is if you surrender the wall and allow those fragile areas to heal and become strong, which is their true nature, those areas of you will become the most capable and dynamic leading forces for your success. So, in short, arrogance is just fear of knowing your true strength.

In our earlier discussion about our beliefs being at the root of all we observe and produce in the world, the discussion would not be complete without the element of surrender. We cannot move forward and claim the fullness of our success without surrendering all that is blocking our more enlightened selves to come forward. Surrender allows us to know ourselves. Without fail, my clients who surrender and allow the fast changes are the ones who go the farthest, with the least amount of effort. Each and every time. Nothing lasting will manifest in your life without surrender.

Surrender Is Not Giving Up

Surrender is not a choice to just be comfortable with what is at the present; that would better define giving up. Be grateful and find joy in each moment, live in the now. And be willing to fully know who you are.

Surrendering Saves Energy

Surrender means not running, not creating elaborate schemes to not have to face ourselves, and not relying solely on coping tools. In fact, coping tools alone are dangerous because they shave off just enough discomfort that we again put our less developed parts on the back burner to be ignored. We have lost that day's opportunity to grow in that area. Eventually those coping tools lose their power once the issue becomes too blatant. The lesson will keep beating down your door until the door is opened. In the end, it is much easier to just open the door. It takes a lot of energy to stay in resistance. Resistance bleeds us dry. Let's save all our energy for more wonderful things in life. If you are like me, having any extra energy is always welcome!

A Teachable Heart Is a Loving Heart

Surrender is never without love. The two are inseparable. I have personally witnessed miraculous changes in lives, including my own, when love for all others becomes available in a person's heart, even for the worst kind of criminal. Your success and self-fulfillment will match your love. It is easy to look successful. It is an entirely different story to have that success and have a fullness of peace and joy with it. Aim for the latter.

Love means seeing all others as beautiful as God sees them. Having a career that pumps you up in the morning entails loving the people who you are involved with serving. This will draw more people to you. And when in life a person is antagonistic toward you, you can just see them as a person struggling, love them, and not be affected by it.

In the fictional story below, "The Angel and the Book," I write on the topic of surrender, humility, and unconditional love. As you will see, the lesson the man is to learn does not let up until he finally learns it. Partial attempts do not satisfy his need for growth. In wisdom, the angel does not remove the discomfort. The choice is ours for how long and painful we want our transformation to be.

 The Angel and the Book

There was a man who lived a very prideful life. Everyone in town avoided him for the shark he was. He had few friends but didn't seem to mind because he had his sights on worldly wealth and counted that as success. He thought he knew better.

Then one day, an angel appeared before the man. On behalf of his love for the man, the angel provided him with the opportunity to release his pride through an invitation of humility and love. The man was frightened and tried to run away. But each time he ran, the angel was there waiting for him. Finally, the man gave up and asked exhaustively,

"Who are you and what do you want from me?" The angel handed him a book. In the book was the answer to his biggest problem.

The man wanted the book very much. With the book, he knew he would learn how to have more wealth. The angel took the book back and said, "You may have the contents of this book under one condition." "What is that?" the man asked. "Tomorrow, find one small way to show kindness and humility. Do it. Then return here telling me of your experience. But there is a warning. Do not do it, and the requirement will be added to."

"That's it?" asked the man. "It sounds very easy. I'll do it, and you will be very impressed."

The man left knowing how easy this was going to be and how he would have the book to solve his greatest problem. In his mind, he was sure this would make him rich.

The next day, the man thought of how much kindness and humility he demonstrated because he bent over and helped a woman retrieve a dropped coin. He made sure others around him saw his humble act as he grasped the coin. Not to mention, he had to get his fingers dirty to pick it out of the dust. Surely this was what the angel was talking about. He was excited to share with the angel his act of humility and retrieve the answer from the book. He could just envision the money and fame coming toward him.

That night the man returned to tell the angel of his great humble act and to retrieve the book.

He excitedly and demonstratively showed the angel how he bent over and gallantly picked up the woman's coin. He even mentioned that he was in a hurry and stopped to help the woman and how his hands became inconveniently dirty.

The man held out his hand to receive the book from the angel. The angel lovingly said, "Tomorrow find two ways to show love for others and humility. Return and tell me, and I will give you the book."

This made the man very angry. "You mean to tell me you will not give me the book to solve my biggest problem after all I did for that woman yesterday?"

The angel just stood still, smiling at the man.

The man was very irritated. Out of pride, he decided he would show this angel how he does not quit and he could surely show humility two times tomorrow.

The next day, the man saw a boy carrying a heavy load. In a booming voice, the man announced that he would carry the load to his destination. He looked around and saw several people watching while he lifted the load to the porch. He reached out his hand and told the boy with a firm hand shake how glad he was he could be of such great service to him and how grateful he must be to have had the load lifted to the porch with his help.

Seeing how well that worked and knowing he had to perform two services, he quickly found another person to carry something for, made sure others around again saw him, incited their gratitude for him and left. The man was now very anxious to tell the angel of his two larger acts of humility. He did get a little sweaty and had to go home to change his shirt. This was surely enough.

Upon telling the angel, the man pantomimed the lifting of the load and added that he got a little sweaty and soiled his white shirt carrying the load. With confidence, the man reached out his hand to take the book.

But again, the angel calmly stood there and told him to find four ways to show humility. The man, wanting the book, conceded in a huff. Day after day, he performed his magnanimous duties of love and humility and returned to the angel and night after night, only to have the angel give him more to do.

At this point the man was livid. He jumped, ranted, screamed, and blamed the angel for all of his problems and frustration. This went on for hours until finally he fell asleep on the ground, completely spent.

In the morning, while dirty, tear-stained, and rumpled, the man stood up. The angel was no longer there. He got up and went into town. He was so tired he didn't care what people thought of him, he only wanted to go home.

On the way home he saw an old man looking confused, not knowing which way to turn to get to the market. The man stopped briefly, and without thinking of the angel or the book, he gave him directions to the bookstore and started to walk off. As the man was walking off, he saw that the elderly man was not making the correct turn. The man walked toward the older gentleman, offered him his arm, and walked with him all the way inside the bookstore. Once inside the store, the man noticed the older gentlemen was having a difficulty choosing a book. Wanting to help, the man sat the elder comfortably in a chair and went about to find something interesting for him to read. While reaching for a book, he felt something he had never quite felt before—a new perspective of true spiritual growth.

He saw the elderly gentleman as perfect. He saw the gentleman's heart. He felt his goodness. He saw his struggles and had compassion. He saw the man as great.

As he retrieved the book from the shelf, his heart cracked open, it was the book from the angel. Turning around, he noticed the old man had left. With the book in his hands, he began to weep. He put the book back on the shelf and walked home. He no longer wanted or needed anything from the book to solve his biggest problem; he had solved it.

Loving all people includes you. Value who you are and what you have to contribute. Trust in the fact that no one can replace you. You are enough. Your call to greatness is expecting you.

Chapter 10

THE GATEWAY TO YOUR DREAM CAREER

"If you find a path with no obstacles,
it probably doesn't lead anywhere."
—Frank A. Clark

Give yourself a big hug and an air high five, for completing this book and making your dream a priority. You are that much closer to your dream-come-true life. This is the process of seeking your true self. It is not for the feebleminded or faint of heart. It takes the perseverance of a bold woman and warrior spirit. It is for the kind of women who in their deepest selves, have somewhere inside always known there is more to life.

In following these six steps of this internal process, you will find you have a compass to keep you going in the right direction—the direction of your heart. Many people try this and feel alone in their personal journey. However, you are fully supported and will feel understood and relieved of the pressure to figure this out alone. This process works. I do want to bring up that when on a journey, roadblocks inevitably appear. So before we walk this path together, I want to give you a heads up.

Change Is Difficult

Change is difficult. That is not a secret. If change were easy, we would all be living our dreams all the time. The individual who can realize her dreams is the one who can tolerate change. There are countless people out there who talk about change, about what they would do differently. But it takes a courageous and malleable soul to be able to surrender what is needed to have what it is they really want. I know that it is hard. I am a witness of the work.

Those who are willing to do the work to improve do best with a mentor or an accountability friend that has been there before to keep you on track. I know I never go at it alone. It takes too long, it's lonely, and it's too painful. Seeking upward change and your truth is about becoming the best version of yourself as possible in this lifetime. It's a lot further than you think.

There Are No Shortcuts

However, Rome was not built in a day. It takes some time to do the work to get where you want to go. The work cannot be skimmed. All the steps must be completed and the journey must be authentic. Skipping processes can undermine your progress. There is no wasted effort or investment in uncovering you. When Michelangelo sculpted David, he said that David was already in the stone. Michelangelo could see the David, and he believed it could be freed from the stone.

Like the David, your future life is already in there. It already exists. You just need to believe it can be uncovered. I have seen the David. It is a wonder to behold, but discovering all that's inside of you is much more elegant and eternally impactful than the most intelligent and artistic piece of art in the world.

Uncovering your talents and gifts brings up a lot of stuff along the way. Many things that you have not seen before as any sort of problem, will be right there in your way like a boulder on your path. What seemed small becomes big and what you think you knew gets turned upside down. It is a rebuilding of yourself.

The clients who get their ducks in a row, get the career of their life, and do it with joy are the ones that make the outcome nonnegotiable. They have made a firm decision that they are masters of their lives. Not completing what they start does not even enter their minds. I have also found that chronic succeeders are consistent in finishing what they start. If you do the work, your life will be more amazing than you can see now. That is certain.

You Must Be Fully Resolved

Doubt will creep in. It is part of the process for anyone wanting to make forward movements in their life and make the changes necessary. In our modern society, you are accepted if you are like this or that. It takes guts to stand up for something. There will be people who will try to keep you the same. These are their own fears. If you change, then they will have to admit that they have something in them to improve as well. It will trigger some reactions and push some buttons in some people. Take this as a sign you are doing just what you are supposed to be doing and are on track.

As women, and this is a point that bears at least mentioning, we have been suppressed in certain ways over thousands of years. Through history, we have been valued for our outward appearance, our ability to bear children, our sensuality, or what have you. Our willingness to conform to societal or cultural demands and to not rock the boat keeps the world in its comfort zone. Over time, our voices have been muted. When women decide to change, it causes the world to change in major ways. It is my belief that all people, male or female, should have the opportunity to be in their true power, one that is in balance with no one in power above the other but in harmony and support of all. Some will applaud you and want to be like you; others may not have that reaction. Like I have said in earlier chapters, if you feel a desire to find yourself in your truth, the world needs you, more than ever.

There Is Another, More Difficult Option

There are two options to choose from when you are stepping up to a new life path. I like to think of Legos in this analogy. We all are familiar with Legos and have probably stepped on a few barefooted in our days of raising young kids. We have all built our life on the last building block. Each decision, circumstance, person, and so on in our life has helped to create which block was added next. Then over the years, we have a Lego land that is the current version of you. Close our eyes for a second and tell yourself what that Lego structure looks like now. Take your time. Write it down. It's kind of fun.

Now there are adventurous spirits who love a challenge in life. They want to move past their current potential. They know that there is more. They want to know who they *really* are. Even if they do not know exactly how to get there, they know their inner self has been whispering for quite some time, and today is the day to listen.

Consider that Lego creation again. Now let's pretend you are exactly where you want to be in life. You have the career that makes a difference in the lives of others, the lives of your family members, and in your own life. You have a life of insight, clarity, and balance. You are living in your full potential. Look at what happens to the Lego structure, let it morph organically in your mind. What has to happen? Are there some layers that need to be taken down and rebuilt? Is there a complete demolition of one side? Is it higher, longer, more intricate? Does it have new colors added? Is it bigger? Is the foundation the same, expanded or is some areas of the foundation look brand new?

Give yourself a few minutes to visualize this. If you have a hard time with visual imaginations, then draw it out with a pencil. Use colors, get creative. However you choose to do this exercise, give yourself the leeway to make it whatever it is. Do not stop it. This is your inner self who knows the bigger picture. Let her drive. What surprised you? What was exciting? What did you learn about yourself? Can you see a metaphor in the design?

The second option is keeping the same Lego structure and trying to build on top of the old foundation. It is much, much harder this way. The outcome will be not what you envision. To me, that is a much more difficult way to live.

Life will challenge you. It is inevitable. Once you begin to move forward, the old things that are there must step aside. There is only room for one or the other. It is almost uncanny how the closer you get to realizing your dreams and your truth, the more stuff will show up. It may seem like a mean joke. But this is God, the Universal Mind, working with you to make sure the job is complete and not left halfway undone.

Embrace the challenges. Understanding these phenomena will make it easier for you to keep going. My clients who get this never quit and reap the reward only those willing to persevere receive. And they take much joy in the process.

This book was written for you as a gateway to your dream life. One that is filled with all the magic you deserve and all the joy and freedom you can hold. It does not happen by thinking about it. It can only manifest with doing the work. Make this the way of living each day, with the intention that you are seeking your highest life path. Do it with all the creativity, love and grace you have. Work it and let it work for you. You can do this or you would not be here. I am here for you. I share this with you because this is my purpose and my joy, to see others find theirs. I have walked this. I have been there in the deepest of ways. One day, you will be able to share your growth with others in your unique way.

If you approach this journey believing that you are not alone in this and you are not doing this only for yourself. You are doing this for all whom you will encounter. Your change will have a ripple effect that you may not see now, but I promise, it will be larger than you think. I honor your journey toward seeking your voice, your truth, your full purpose for being here on earth. There is nothing more powerful than being strong for someone else, but in order to fully do that, you must do your work first.

The Higher Price of Not Following Through

Fear of failure is the number-one real reason people do not move forward in finding their dreams just as the fear of loss prevents some from declaring their love for another. We are not genuine in these emotional places. The irony is that that those who hold back end up with exactly what they feared the most.

The price is very high when we do not give ourselves permission to be our best selves. Taking the road of least resistance may feel easy now, but easy now is hard later. Not accepting the call gets very expensive because the truth is unable to be hidden completely. It takes a lot of energy to constantly push down our potential. Energy that could otherwise be directed and employed for excelling at our purpose in life.

When all of your energy can be put directly into use toward your purpose and not in trying to hide, miracles happen and they happen in a more effortless way. Things come toward you, and you move toward the people you are called to serve.

We are more afraid of our light than we are of our darkness. Marianne Williamson said it better than anyone.

"Our deepest fear is not that we are inadequate. Our deepest fear is that we are powerful beyond measure. It is our Light, not our Darkness, that most frightens us."

CONCLUSION

In my experience working with clients, I am going to make a stab that in our relationship to this point, you think the work here is great, but you don't feel you are far enough along in the process—that is, at least to the level that you know it can be, that it ought to be.

I'm going to guess that you are hoping you are not like the dozens of women you know and have seen who are not excited about what jobs they can find conveniently, and that is not what they would put up on their dream board. I'm also guessing that at this point of your process, to be like the dozens of women you know that, in the end, decide to forfeit their dream, or tell themselves they do not have one, to make others more comfortable makes you extremely uncomfortable.

Go back to that note you wrote in the start of the book of how you are feeling today about actualizing your dreams. Has that intensified, changed? Whatever it is, honor and observe it. It is part of what has gotten you here today. It is also a big clue to an internal working point to further your development. Nothing is without significance.

Action and Decision

It is action and decision to live intentionally that makes life happen. Think if you were seeing a two-year-old walking too close to a busy street. It is crazy to think you would ponder on what to do. Should I call for him? See if he turns back on his own? How close will he get? No, you would run after the baby as quickly as you could, whisk him up in your arms and carry him back to safety. And it wouldn't matter whose baby it was. You would just take action to save his life.

Results come by those who act while others are trying to figure things out. I wrote this book and created the Explore and Discover Your Purpose system immediately after I knew this was the way to serve my highest purpose. There is nothing to try to figure out; you just act on the next step in front of you. You can only make changes while you are in movement.

The universe greatly rewards those who take action on what is being provided.

One thing I have learned through my journey to find my highest life path is that I used to think I was the one searching for it. But in actuality, it was my path searching for me. Your career wants you so badly. The people you are going to help are waiting for you. And you will move closer to it with each action to connect with it. Mindful action makes the difference—mindful action with your heart centered on stepping up to your greatness. It's a calling. It's taking the hero's journey.

As a master transformation coach, the goal is to significantly speed up the growth with an environment of love, support, and masterminding for light-years of spiritual progress catered exactly to you. Some people prefer to work their challenges on their own and do not want their life discovery and career path to be moved along that quickly. At Explore and Discover Your Purpose, the importance is on compassion, speed and individuality.

The Explore and Discover Client

I chose binoculars for the cover because it represents a person who is willing to look far into what is possible for them. That is the person who stays curious and who finds great treasures, has fuller clarity and depth to life. The joy is that by putting up the binoculars, what you actually discover is a deeper and more whole you.

Explore and Discover Clients

- Know they have more inside of them to be expressed
- Fear that not finding their personal gifts and a career is choosing a life of quiet desperation
- Know they will not let what has been building and burning inside them go unfinished and undiscovered
- Value speed and are people who sees themselves as women of action
- Want to feel safe, confident, nurtured and have joy while finding their career
- Sees investing in themselves as the best way to give to everyone else.

Never let anyone discourage you from taking this next step in life that you know is right for you. The right career path can improve your entire life, the life of your family, and the lives of all those whom you touch. You will feel complete and that the ripple effect is real and can create lasting change.

Let yourself find out. What will it look like when I know what it is I'm supposed to be doing now? When you find that, life will happen in a whole new way. You will never be left wondering. You will know.

TEN BELIEFS AT EXPLORE AND DISCOVER YOUR PURPOSE TRANSFORMATION

1. Each person on this journey to a life and career of meaning has a purpose inside unique to them.
2. Spiritual development and finding your purpose are fundamental to why we are here.
3. A life of intention to continually grow brings joy, fulfillment, and peace on all fronts.
4. Finding a way to earn your own income gives you more freedom and power to give and serve.
5. My absolute focus is on serving you specifically and facilitating where your highest self knows it's supposed to go.
6. Everyone has the right to choose their path and to find their own purpose.

7. I deliver fast results for clients and work as quickly as you are capable and desire to move you forward to your success.

8. Your career is more than a career, everything has a higher purpose and meaning.

9. It is necessary to be a little uncomfortable and leave the comfort zone to progress.

10. I provide safety, patience and compassion and hold space at all stages of the process to your personal goals.

ACKNOWLEDGMENTS

I vividly remember the day I learned to read. I felt empowered and free, like I had the universe in my grasp. I stood and read the words for my family with confidence and elation. Danny and the Dinosaur and Frog and Toad are Friends gave me joy, excitement, and ignited my imagination. I could slide down the dinosaur's back and stand on my head to think of a story to tell Frog. I still have those same book copies in my cabinet today, along with many others from my early childhood. I thank my mom for saving those books, reading Jack and the Bean Stalk to me with full animation, buying so many Scholastic books with the school, and for all the trips back and forth to the public library, which were many.

This book idea came together as a result of a persistent and loving whispering in my heart that there is specific book waiting to be written. Although I officially started writing this book only four months before its publishing date, I really began writing it three years ago. One day, out of nowhere, there began a flood of creative stories that poured out of me as if I had been writing my entire life, which I hadn't. Seeing now how these stories helped to write this book and how the book process was all in divine right order is both humbling and confirming. Life is very fun and fulfilling when you allow it to be!

As it is in all things, there are many people who have played a part in the writing and support of this book. To the folks who trusted me and signed up to work with me when I was brand new as a transformation coach and intuitive mentor and to the powerhouse clients who make my work a sheer joy in life, hats off and my deepest respect. To Bill Phipps for his genius and his devoted hours on the phone with me runs deep. To Mark Januszewski for giving me a reason to start a blog. To Angela Lauria and her team for making this a reality.

To my husband, Rhett, of 26 years for seeing straight into my heart, being my soul mate and holding space for me to grow. To my all of my children, Ty, Van, Ryan, Morgan, Luke, Mackenzie and the rest coming for the inspiration, love and deeper meaning to life. To my dad for always believing, loving, and telling me that I can. I would not feel complete if I did not include my uncle for his genuineness and hope in me always, including to write this book.

To the Morgan James Publishing team: Special thanks to David Hancock, CEO & Founder for believing in me and my message. To my Author Relations Manager, Margo Toulouse, thanks for making the process seamless and easy. Many more thanks to everyone else, but especially Jim Howard, Bethany Marshall, and Nickcole Watkins.

And to you for believing in yourself enough to read this book! If you are reading this, you are officially exploring and discovering your purpose. What next then? If you choose to take the transformation to butterfly and see what the sky has to offer is up to you. I hope you do. The world needs the part only you can fulfill.

ABOUT THE AUTHOR

 Marlo Andersen is the founder of the Explore and Discover Your Purpose System for finding a career that has meaning and depth. She has helped many clients uncover what it is they are uniquely designed to do in life, even when they had no idea of these gifts before they began working with her.

Marlo has been in private practice as a transformation coach, healer and intuitive mentor since 2010. Skilled in a wide range of healing and energy modalities to richly serve her clients, she leaves no stone unturned. Her work focuses on uncovering her clients' true self, personal power, and fullest purposes in life. She serves to greatly accelerate an otherwise long process of day-to-day personal development and evolution, so her clients can enjoy the furthest reaching results out of life and career

For more information, email Marlo@marloandersen.com or find Marlo on Facebook at www.facebook.com/marlo.andersen.

THANK YOU

Thank you for reading!

FREE COMPANION VIDEO SERIES

I've created a video series as a companion to this book, which a can be found at www.ExploreandDiscoverYourPurpose.com/videos. If you want to know more about how to find your dream career and live a full life using all of your superpowers, check it out and let me know what you think on Facebook.

You can find me on Facebook at www.facebook.com/marlo.andersen or email me at marlo@marloandersen.com